Also by Jaroslaw Jankowski

Why Are We So Different?
Your Guide to the 16 Personality Types

Why are we so very different from one another?
Why do we organise our lives in such disparate
ways? Why are our modes of assimilating
information so varied? Why are our approaches
to decision-making so diverse? Why are our
forms of relaxing and 'recharging our batteries'
so dissimilar?

Your Guide to the 16 Personality Types will help you
to understand both yourselves and other people
better. It will aid you not only in avoiding any
number of traps, but also in making the most of
your personal potential, as well as in taking the
right decisions about your education and career
and in building healthy relationships with others.
The book contains the ID16™© Personality
Test, which will enable you to determine your
own personality type. It also offers
a comprehensive description of each of the
sixteen types.

The Director

Your Guide
to the ENTJ Personality Type

The ID16^{TM©} Personality Types series

JAROSLAW JANKOWSKI
M.Ed., EMBA

LOGOS MEDIA

This is a book which can help you exploit your potential more fully, build healthy relationships with other people and make the right decisions about your education and career. However, it should not be considered to be a substitute for expert physiological or psychiatric consultation. Neither the author nor the publisher accept any responsibility whatsoever for any detrimental effects which may result from the inappropriate use of this book.

ID16™© is an independent typology developed by Polish educator and manager Jaroslaw Jankowski and grounded in Carl Gustav Jung's theory. It should not be confused with the personality typologies and tests proposed by other authors or offered by other institutions.

Original title: Twój typ osobowości: Dyrektor (ENTJ)
Translated from the Polish by Caryl Swift
Proof reading: Lacrosse | experts in translation
Layout editing by Zbigniew Szalbot

Published by LOGOS MEDIA

Paperback: ISBN 978-83-7981-063-5
EPUB: ISBN 978-83-7981-064-2
MOBI: ISBN 978-83-7981-065-9

Contents

Preface

The work in your hands is a compendium of knowledge on the *director*. It forms part of the *ID16™© Personality Types* series, which consists of sixteen books on the individual personality types and *Who Are You? The ID16™© Personality Test*, an introduction to the ID16™© independent personality typology, which is based on the theory developed by Carl Gustav Jung.

As you explore this book on the *director*, you will find the answer to a number of crucial questions:

- How do *directors* think and what do they feel? How do they make decisions? How do they solve problems? What makes them anxious? What do they fear? What irritates them?
- Which personality types are they happy to encounter on their road through life and

which ones do they avoid? What kind of friends, life partners and parents do they make? How do others perceive them?

- What are their vocational predispositions? What sort of work environment allows them to function most effectively? Which careers best suit their personality type?
- What are their strengths and what do they need to work on? How can they make the most of their potential and avoid pitfalls?
- Which famous people correspond to the *director*'s profile?

The book also contains the most essential information about the ID16™© typology.

We sincerely hope that it will help you in coming to know yourself and others better.

ID16™© and Jungian Personality Typology

ID16™© numbers among what are referred to as Jungian personality typologies, which draw on the theories developed by Carl Gustav Jung (1875-19161), a Swiss psychiatrist and psychologist and a pioneer of the 'depth psychology' approach.

On the basis of many years of research and observation, Jung came to the conclusion that the differences in people's attitudes and preferences are far from random. He developed a concept which is highly familiar to us today: the division of people into extroverts and introverts. In addition, he distinguished four personality functions, which form two opposing pairs: sensing-intuition and thinking-feeling. He also established that one function is dominant in each pair. He became convinced that each and every person's dominant functions are fixed and independent of external conditions and that, together, what they form is a personality type.

In 1938, two American psychiatrists, Horace Gray and Joseph Wheelwright, created the first personality test based on Jung's theories. It was designed to make it possible to determine the dominant functions within the three dimensions described by Jung, namely, **extraversion-introversion**, **sensing-intuition** and **thinking-feeling**. That first test became the inspiration for other researchers. In 1942, again in America, Isabel Briggs Myers and Katherine Briggs began using their own personality test, broadening Gray's and Wheelwright's classic, three-dimensional model to include a fourth: **judging-perceiving**. The majority of subsequent personality typologies and tests drawing on Jung's theories also take that fourth dimension into account. They include the American typology published by David W. Keirsey in 1978 and the personality test developed in the nineteen seventies by Aušra Augustinavičiūtė, a Lithuanian psychologist. Over the following decades, other European researchers followed in their footsteps, creating more four-dimensional personality typologies and tests for use in personal coaching and career counselling.

ID16$^{TM©}$ figures among that group. An independent typology developed by Polish educator and manager Jaroslaw Jankowski, it was published in the first decade of the twenty-first century. ID16$^{TM©}$ is based on Carl Jung's classic theory and, like other contemporary Jungian typologies, it follows a four-dimensional path, terming those dimensions the **four natural inclinations**. These inclinations are dichotomous in nature and the picture they provide gives us information regarding a person's personality type. Analysis of the first inclination is intended to determine the dominant **source of life energy**, this being either the exterior or the interior world. Analysis of the second inclination defines the dominant **mode of assimilating information**, which occurs via the senses or via intuition. Analysis of the third inclination supplies a description of the **decision-making mode**, where either mind or heart is dominant, while analysis of the fourth inclination produces a definition of the dominant **lifestyle** as either organised or spontaneous. The combination of all these natural inclinations results in **sixteen possible personality types**.

One remarkable feature of the ID16™© typology is its practical dimension. It describes the individual personality types in action – at work, in daily life and in interpersonal relations. It neither concentrates on the internal dynamics of personality nor does it undertake any theoretical attempts at explaining or commenting on invisible, interior processes. The focus is turned more toward the ways in which a given personality type manifests itself externally and how it affects the surrounding world. This emphasis on the social aspect of personality places ID16™© somewhat closer to the previously mentioned typology developed by Aušra Augustinavičiūtė.

Each of the ID16™© personality types is the result of a given person's natural inclinations.

There is nothing evaluative or judgemental about ascribing a person to a given type, though. No particular personality type is 'better' or 'worse' than any other. Each type is quite simply different and each has its own potential strengths and weaknesses. ID16™© makes it possible to identify and describe those differences. It helps us to understand ourselves and discover our place in the world.

Familiarity with our personality profile enables us to make full use of our potential and work on the areas which might cause us trouble. It is an invaluable aid in everyday life, in solving problems, in building healthy relationships with other people and in making decisions relating to our education and careers.

Determining personality is a process which is neither arbitrary nor mechanical in nature. As the 'owner and user' of our personality, each and every one of us is fully capable of defining which type we belong to. The individual's role is thus pivotal. This self-identification can be achieved either by analysing the descriptions of the ID16™© personality types and steadily narrowing down the fields of choice or by taking the short cut provided by the ID16™© Personality Test.[1] The role played by each 'personality user' is equally crucial when it comes to the test, given that the outcome depends entirely on the answers they provide.

---

[1] The test can be found in *Why Are We So Different? Your Guide to the 16 Personality Types* by Jaroslaw Jankowski.

Identifying personality types helps us to know both ourselves and others. Nonetheless, it should not be treated as some kind of future-determining oracle. No personality type can ever justify our weaknesses or poor interpersonal relationships. It might, however, help us to understand their causes!

ID16™© treats personality type not as a static, genetic, pre-determined condition, but as a product of innate and acquired characteristics. As such, it is a concept which neither diminishes free will nor engages in pigeonholing people. What it does is open up new perspectives for us, encouraging us to work on ourselves and indicating the areas where that work is most needed.

The Director (ENTJ)

The Personality in a Nutshell

Life motto: I'll tell you what you need to do.

In brief, *directors* …

are independent, active and decisive. Rational, logical and creative, when they analyse problems they look at the wider picture and are able to foresee the future consequences of human activities. They are characterised by optimism and a healthy sense of their own worth and are capable of transforming theoretical concepts into concrete, practical plans of action.

Visionaries, mentors and organisers, *directors* possess natural leadership skills. Their powerful personalities and direct and critical style can often have an intimidating effect, causing them problems in their interpersonal relationships.

The *director's* four natural inclinations:

- source of life energy: the exterior world
- mode of assimilating information: intuition
- decision-making mode: the mind
- lifestyle: organised

Similar personality types:

- the Innovator
- the Strategist
- the Logician

Statistical data:

- *directors* constitute between two and five per cent of the global community
- men predominate among *directors* (70 per cent)
- Holland is an example of a nation corresponding to the *director's* profile[2]

The Four-Letter Code

In terms of Jungian personality typology, the universal four-letter code for the *director* is ENTJ.

---

[2] What this means is not that all the residents of Holland fall within this personality type, but that Dutch society as a whole possesses a great many of the character traits typical of the *director*.

General character traits

Directors are independent, active and energetic. Their intuition is their guide and they have great faith in it. They are shrewd and clear-headed, with the ability to relate disparate facts and formulate apt generalisations. When tackling problems, they analyse them from various angles and take the broad view.

Perception and thinking

Directors are quick to spot shifts in their surroundings and changing circumstances. Being exceptionally logical and rational, they excel at assessing a situation coolly, objectively and impartially. They think ahead, taking various possible scenarios into consideration and making the most of their ability to foresee the long-term consequences of a given course of action. Optimists by nature, they believe in their own capabilities and assume that they will succeed in doing whatever they undertake to do. This does not make them dreamers, though. On the contrary, they are very well aware of the effort required to accomplish the task in question. They prefer preparing thoroughly before tackling a job and cannot abide improvisation.

Decisions

Directors have the ability to transform theoretical and general concepts into concrete plans of action. They are visionaries and their vision serves them as a shot of energy and a motivating force. When faced with the necessity of making a decision, they like to have time to think it through, weighing up the various possibilities and then selecting the ones that seem to them to be the most logical and rational. Once the decision is made, they roll up their sleeves and get going without further ado.

As others see them

Other people perceive *directors* as powerful personalities, energetic, firm and decisive. They are widely appreciated as reliable and hard-working, though they can also have a reputation for being rather unapproachable and difficult to get close to. Their directness frequently intimidates and even antagonises or alienates others and they are sometimes deemed to be overly critical and demanding. Indeed, on occasion, their colleagues or their nearest and dearest will complain that satisfying them completely is "next to impossible".

Interior compass

Directors are highly independent, following neither prevailing views nor general trends. Their own thoughts and conclusions count for more with them than the opinions of other people and whether or not others share their convictions is a matter of indifference to them. They are strongly wedded to their own principles and outlook and present their opinions and viewpoints as something patently obvious.

As a rule, *directors* assume in advance that they are right and, indeed, that assumption often proves to be correct! Nonetheless, they are capable of verifying their views in the light of new data or changing circumstances. They like challenges and find repetitive and routine activities tedious to a fault. Being of an enquiring disposition, when a concept interests them they make an effort to go into it thoroughly and understand it properly, as well as giving thought to the possibilities of putting it to practical use. In general, they will acquire a wide range of interests in their youth and, over the course of time, will enrich and systemise their knowledge, constructing an internal map of the world which is completely their own and enables them to comprehend reality and the phenomena that occur in it.

Organisational modes

Directors have a tremendous thirst for knowledge and will pose themselves questions and then seek the answers to them. Identifying cause-and-effect relationships comes easily to them, as does discerning the principles which govern the world and human behaviour. Rational arguments are what carry weight with them and they have zero tolerance for logical inconsistency or incoherence in a concept, internal contradictions in a system and overlapping areas of authority, not to mention inefficiency, in an organisation. They have a remarkable love of order and dislike wastefulness and chaos.

Perfectionists by nature, *directors* are quite capable of working incessantly to improve everything they come into contact with. They make highly effective use of their time and have an inbuilt ability for multitasking; watching television and reading a book at one and the same time, for instance, is a piece of cake for them. When they undertake a task, they endeavour to carry it out in the best possible way; consciously doing anything to less than their full capabilities is completely beyond them. They see things through to the end and successfully finishing a job gives them a sense of satisfaction – and liberation, since they are then free to involve themselves in the next task!

Attitude to others

Directors are exceptionally independent, assertive and immune to attempts to manipulate or pressurise them. Other people's criticism rolls off them like water off a duck's back. They are quite capable of saying 'no' and will not allow themselves to be used. When they are convinced of something, the thoughts of others on the subject are of no concern to them whatsoever, although they do make an exception in the case of prominent figures and authorities who enjoy widespread recognition.

They often demonstrate a dismal failure when it comes to comprehending opinions that oppose their own. Discerning other people's feelings is also problematic for them and they are normally unaware of the fact that their critical remarks and bluntly expressed opinions are frequently hurtful to the person at whom they are levelled.

Leisure

Directors are titanic workers and generally incapable of relaxing. Passive leisure is foreign to their nature and even if they happen not to be engaged in a physical activity, their brains will be beavering away nineteen to the dozen, constantly analysing new possibilities and ideas and pondering over how to turn them into reality. They enjoy learning new things and broadening their horizons, so they will happily spend their free time augmenting their knowledge and acquiring new information.

In the face of stress

In the face of prolonged periods of stress, *directors* will sometimes lose faith in themselves and become highly critical of their own achievements. At that stage, they tend to feel swamped by their responsibilities and duties, as well as fearing that they have lost control of the situation. In their efforts to relieve their stress, they may then turn to using substances.

Socially

Directors rarely show their own emotions and are rather sparing in their praise, often coming across as cold, reserved and unapproachable. In reality, though, they are capable of opening up to people to whom they have given their trust.

They can also be highly sentimental and sensitive, despite giving no outward sign of what they are feeling. Indeed, those around them have difficulty in discerning that aspect of their personality – or even, perhaps, in believing that it exists at all!

The company *directors* value most highly is that of intelligent and competent people from whom they can learn something. They respect those who are able to prove the legitimacy of their arguments and can both support their own convictions and defend them vigorously. By the same token, they will often ignore people who fail to rise to that challenge, since they have no grasp of the fact that not everyone shares their relish for disputes and confrontations, but wrongly assume that the inability to voice one's beliefs openly and an unwillingness to fight in defence of one's reasoning is tantamount to a lack of personal points of view.

Directors expect rational and sensible behaviour from others and are incapable of understanding those who are guided by anything other than logic. They dislike repeating themselves and, if other people reject their viewpoint at the outset, they will make no effort to convince them otherwise. They prize freedom, which is why they will sometimes avoid relationships which place limits on their independence. They themselves accord freedom to others and have no inclination to be invasive.

Amongst friends

Contrary to the suppositions of many, good relationships with others matter greatly to *directors*. However, they operate on the premise that any such relationship should serve a concrete purpose, such as solving problems, for instance, or carrying out tasks or helping others to discover their potential.

Spending time amongst people infuses *directors* with energy and they will most readily strike up a friendship with those who share their outlook and convictions or who will broaden their horizons by providing them with new information and experiences. Other people also perceive them as interesting conversationalists and are often inspired and spurred into action by an encounter with them. However, some people are either intimidated or antagonised and alienated by their self-assurance and the firmness with which they voice their views. These two aspects of their character are often taken as arrogance, especially since they usually say what they think, heedless of the circumstances and the feelings of others. They are often just as direct in their questions, which distresses or embarrasses a great many of the people they talk to, some of whom, overwhelmed by their categoric statements, find themselves incapable of voicing their views or thoughts in their presence.

Directors themselves feel absolutely at home in the company of other strong personalities, even when their opinions differ. They appreciate people who are capable of articulating their convictions clearly and have no fear of confrontation. They most often make friends with *innovators*, *strategists*, *administrators* and other *directors*, but struggle to find a common language with *artists*, *presenters* and *protectors*.

As life partners

Directors take their responsibilities in a life partnership extremely seriously. Within the family, they will normally assume the role of leader and sentinel. Actions speak loudest to them, so they show their devotion not so much by way of tender gestures and warm words as through doing something concrete.

Their nature renders them both very insensitive to their partner's feelings and completely unaware of their emotional needs; they may love them dearly and yet, at one and the same time, have absolutely no grasp whatsoever of what they are experiencing and feeling or of their emotional state. However, with a little effort, they can change this and if they are in a relationship with a person of romantic disposition, then making that effort is an absolute must! *Directors* themselves have few emotional needs. They like to know that they are important to, and loved by, their life partner, but they do not, as a rule, expect endearing words, compliments and frequent assurances of love and affection. Their devotion and sense of responsibility for their family is a strong bonding element in their relationships.

Mutual respect is a characteristic feature of *directors'* life partnerships, as is supporting one another's personal growth. They value a relationship which serves as their mainstay and inspiration, and if it stops living up to their expectations they will often walk away from it. Another potential threat is their propensity for workaholism. Usually successful in their professional lives, they are sought-after employees. In many cases they will frequently be away from home and, when they actually are there, will often be absorbed in work-related matters, a state of affairs which normally gives rise to all kinds of tension. The positive attitude *directors* have towards confrontations, disputes and criticism, which they view as factors conducive to self-development and learning, can be a serious problem for romantically inclined and sensitive partners.

The natural candidates for a *director's* life partner are people of a personality type akin to their own: *innovators*, *strategists* or *logicians*. Nonetheless, experience has taught us that people are also capable of creating happy and successful relationships despite what would seem to be an evident typological incompatibility. Moreover, the differences between two partners can lend added dynamics to a relationship and engender personal development. Indeed, to *directors*, this is a prospect that appears more attractive than the vision of a harmonious relationship in which concord and full, mutual understanding hold sway.

As parents

Directors take their role as a parent just as seriously as their life partnership. They help their children to understand the world, teaching them to think for themselves, nurturing their development and placing great emphasis on their education. However, they also make heavy demands of them, as well as expecting respect, obedience and compliance with the rules they set. In extreme cases, they might adopt a high-handed attitude or even operate like overbearing dictators. As a rule, they are unstinting in their criticism of their offspring, but reserved in their praise, and they are also often unperceptive of their emotional needs.

Directors are usually impatient with their children's repeated mistakes and oversights, while sometimes failing to perceive that their expectations go beyond what a child is capable of and that, when the results are poor, this may not be the outcome of laziness, thoughtlessness or a frivolous attitude. Their offspring normally strive to live up to their expectations and avoid inadvertences in order to escape being exposed to their criticism. However, with puberty, a time of crisis often emerges; at that stage, teenage children cease to accept their *director* parent's rules and usually revolt against their discipline and regulations. *Directors* themselves struggle to come to terms with their offspring's ever burgeoning independence.

When *directors* succeed in avoiding those mistakes, they are superb parents and excellent figures of authority to their children. They are also instrumental in their development, encouraging them to explore the world, acquire knowledge and face up to challenges. As a result, their offspring usually grow up to become responsible, creative and independent adults with no fear of taking up the gauntlets that life throws at their feet.

Work and career paths

Their professional career is a vital element of *directors'* lives and they are generally devoted to their work and frequently ascend to the highest of posts.

Quick to identify new challenges and problems, they are just as fast in tackling them and equally swift when it comes to spotting potential and doing something about it. Their thinking is global and far-reaching and they are visionaries, first delineating their goals and then applying themselves zealously to accomplishing them. When seeking solutions, they usually take the long-term view; their thinking goes beyond the current situation and they have the ability to foresee factors which may appear in the future. All of this, combined with their reliability, responsibility and predisposition for hard work, makes them sought-after employees. They are able to devote all their energy to accomplishing tasks they believe in. On the other hand, they are incapable of committing themselves wholeheartedly to undertakings which they believe to be unrealistic, fuzzy or incoherent.

Views on workplace hierarchy

Directors appreciate competent superiors who have got where they are on merit and have concrete achievements under their belt. They also value those who give their subordinates freedom in carrying out the tasks assigned to them.

As part of a team

When *directors* work as part of a team, they seize the initiative and, willingly or not, take responsibility on their shoulders. As such, they are perceived as natural leaders and, indeed, where they go, others will follow. They have the ability to motivate other people and put them in the frame of mind to achieve the goals that have been set, firing them with optimism and faith in their success. They are also capable of drawing out the best in others and of helping them realise their potential. However, their method of assistance is extremely unlikely to involve providing ready-made solutions or doing everything for them; as a rule, they will throw people in at the deep end.

Superb mentors and coaches, they assist people in identifying their long-term aims and then transforming them into short-term action plans. In positions of authority, they keep their subordinates informed both of impending changes in their environment and of future challenges, and they keep a firm eye on the effectiveness and efficiency of the company or the department for which they are responsible.

Tasks

When *directors* begin work on an undertaking, they define the measures necessary to accomplish it and then find the right people to carry it out while they move on, eager to devote themselves to the next new task. They are excellent at handling the kind of complex problems which other people are only too happy to avoid like the plague and are also good strategists, with the ability to define priorities with pinpoint accuracy.

Companies and institutions

Directors fit in well in corporations and businesses which provide prospects for promotion, apply clear rules for the game and reward their employees for concrete achievements. On the other hand, they will be restless and unhappy in companies where compliance with the accepted regulations or detailed procedures takes precedence over creative ideas and results.

Work style

Directors make for ideal managers in fields demanding organisational skills and strategic planning, such as creating new systems from scratch or implementing innovative solutions, organising teams and managing companies in the throes of transformation. Their ability to multitask means that they are also capable of coordinating a host of different ventures and projects at one and the same time.

They will very often make it to the very top of their company's hierarchical tree and are thus often directors … hence the name for this personality type. They like working with people they can rely on and who fulfil the tasks assigned to them, sharing their enthusiasm and zeal for work with them. By the same token, they find passiveness, lethargy and a lack of commitment intolerable. Impatient with those who fail to keep pace, drag out their tasks or continually make the same mistakes, they are capable of being direct, sometimes to the point of brutal frankness, when evaluating their achievements, paying no regard to the fact that they might hurt or offend them. They also have no difficulty in parting company with employees who fail to live up to their expectations. Other people's feelings are rarely a matter of concern to them; making the right decision matters more to them than winning and keeping the favour of those around them. A want of order, waste, excessive bureaucracy and overly complex procedures all irritate them immensely.

When *directors* look at problems, they do so objectively, with no concern for sentimental or emotional considerations. They have no attachment to particular solutions either, and are ready to discard them the moment they fail to perform as required. Who introduced them and how long they have been in place is of no great significance to them and they are capable of coldly eliminating any that are impractical or ineffective. Indeed, they are able do away with time-honoured work methods, practices and habits in one fell swoop and, when they are convinced that their ideas are the way forward, they may well set out to accomplish them at any price – by violating procedures and paying no heed at all to the human cost.

Professions

Knowledge of our own personality profile and natural preferences provides us with invaluable help in choosing the optimal path in our professional careers. Experience has shown that, while *directors* are perfectly able to work and find fulfilment in a range of fields, their personality type naturally predisposes them to the following fields and professions:

- administrator
- artistic director
- CEO
- computer systems analyst
- credit analyst
- development director
- entrepreneur

- executive director
- human resources
- IT specialist
- journalist
- judge
- lawyer
- life coach
- loans and credit
- manager
- marketing
- marketing director
- musician
- politician
- project coordinator
- investor
- psychologist
- public administration
- public relations
- scientist
- urban / rural planning
- tertiary educator
- writer

Potential strengths and weaknesses

Like any other personality type, *directors* have their potential strengths and weaknesses and this potential can be cultivated in a variety of ways. *Directors'* personal happiness and professional fulfilment depend on whether they make the most of the 'pluses' offered by their personality type and face up to its inherent dangers. Here, then is a SUMMARY of those 'pluses' and dangers:

Potential strengths

Directors have a healthy sense of their own worth and possess natural leadership skills. Capable of firing others with optimism and faith in their success, they themselves brim with energy, enthusiasm for work and the ability to put their whole heart into accomplishing tasks they believe in. Their vision gives them energy and they are thus able to work extremely hard in order to accomplish it. They are characterised by a positive attitude to tasks and problems, being well aware of the potential difficulties but believing that they will succeed in meeting the challenge. With their serious approach to their responsibilities, one thing is certain: once they take on a job, they will see it through to the end. Fresh concepts and ideas interest them and they are open to new solutions, possessing the ability to assimilate them and apply them when accomplishing their own tasks.

Independent, active and creative, they have the ability to transform theoretical and general concepts into concrete plans of action. They approach their work very seriously and expect the same of others. Their focus is on the merits of the matter and they refuse to allow less crucial aspects to distract them. When analysing facts and data, they are cool and objective, giving emotion and bias short shrift. They are able to manage money and other resources effectively and efficiently and are well-organised and extremely hard-working, as well as being direct and straightforward; no one will ever need to spend time wondering what their opinion on a given topic might be. *Directors* say what they think. They are good oral communicators and public speaking and debate pose no major problems for them.

By nature, they are interested in self-development, acquiring knowledge and self-improvement in various areas of their lives. With their powerful, assertive personality, they cope well in difficult situations of conflict and are capable of putting an end to friendships and acquaintanceships if they become uncomfortable or destructive. They are open to constructive criticism. Given their love of order, they make superb organisers, as well as excelling in orchestrating the work of others, having a flair for creating systems which function effectively and efficiently and being good strategists, with the ability to define priorities with pinpoint accuracy.

Potential weaknesses

Directors pursue confrontation. Their love of tough polemics and dispute means that they are seen as difficult and critical conversationalists, while their powerful personalities often have an intimidating effect on others and can even arouse anxieties and fears. When they argue a point with other people, they strive to prove that they are absolutely right and completely 'wipe the floor' with their opponents; rarely will they be able to admit that someone who holds a different view could be right, even if only in part. They have difficulty in understanding the needs of others when they differ from their own and, by their very nature, are insensitive to other people's feelings and reactions. Expressing their own feelings and emotions comes just as hard to them and they are at rather a loss in situations demanding that they read those of others. They fare no better when it comes to listening, and have a tendency to criticise any opinion whatsoever if it fails to concur with their own point of view.

Highly demanding of themselves, they are no more sparing in the high standards they require others to meet, even though they generally set the benchmark too high for many. When they call other people's attention to wastefulness, perfunctoriness or other oversights, they are often extremely severe and can even be harsh to the point of roughness. At the same time, they are very stinting in their praise when things are going well, setting no store by positive reinforcement in the form of encouragement, approval and rewards. Seizing the initiative comes naturally to them and they are reluctant to share responsibility with others, as well as displaying a frequent tendency to make premature and ill-considered decisions. In extreme cases, their pursuit of authority can see them acting dogmatically and high-handedly towards those they seek to oversee; on occasion, they may well even humiliate them. When they find themselves in stressful situations, they are liable to explode in anger and manifest other forms of aggressive behaviour. They may also endeavour to relieve their tension by overeating or abusing alcohol.

The dogmatism and extremely rational approach to life exhibited by directors, together with their inability to identify other people's needs, are all characteristics which often cause them problems and can lead to a specific form of social isolation, whereby they are highly valued at work but have no friends to speak of. With no real grasp as to why this should be, they will sometimes begin to suspect other people of wishing them ill or conspiring against them. Those who are either incapable of adapting to their ideas and plans or have no wish to do so are another frequent source of frustration to them.

Personal development

Directors' personal development depends on the extent to which they make use of their natural potential and surmount the dangers inherent in their personality type. What follows are some practical tips which, together, form a specific guide that we might call *The Director's Ten Commandments.*

Admit that you can make mistakes

Things may be more complex than they seem to you. You may not always be in the right. Bring that thought to the forefront of your mind before you start accusing others or pointing out their mistakes and reproaching them.

Criticise less

Not everyone is able to handle constructive criticism. In fact, dispensing it frankly can have a destructive effect in many cases. Studies have shown that praising positive behaviour, albeit limited, motivates people more than criticising negative conduct.

Praise more

Make the most of every occasion to appreciate other people, say something nice to them and praise them for something they have done. At work, value people not only for the job they do, but also for who they are. Then wait and see. The difference will come as a pleasant surprise!

Stop trying to control absolutely everything

Eagerness to control everything will only lead to your eventual frustration. Keep your eye on the most important things and leave less crucial matters to others – or even just let them run their own course.

Listen to people

Show an interest in other people, even when you disagree with them or are convinced that they are wrong. Save your response until you have heard them out. The ability to listen could well revolutionise your relationship with others.

Stop blaming others for your problems

Your problems may not only be caused by others; they might also be caused by you! You, too, are capable of oversights and mistakes. You, too, can be the root of a problem.

Treat others kindly

People want to be treated as something more than simply the performers of tasks. They long for their emotions, feelings and enthusiasms to be perceived. Mix with people, communicate with them, try to put yourself in their shoes and understand what they are going through, what fascinates them, what worries them and what they fear.

Control your emotions

If you feel that you might well explode, then try to relax, wind down and think about something else for a moment. Outbursts of anger help neither you nor the people around you.

Be more understanding

Show others more warmth. Remember that not everyone should be assigned the same tasks, because not everyone is skilled in the same fields. If others are unable to cope with a task, this is not always a sign of their ill will or laziness.

Learn to take things easy

Taking time out is not synonymous with wasting precious hours, minutes and seconds and there is no legislation requiring you to feel guilty if you set work to one side and relax or do something for the sheer pleasure of it. What will actually happen is that your batteries will be recharged in the process; and that can only make you more efficient and effective at work!

Well-known figures

Below is a list of some well-known people who match the *director's* profile:

- **Jack London** (John Griffith Chaney; 1876-1916); an American writer whose works include *The Call of the Wild*, he was also a naturalist and was deemed one of the most romantic figures of his time.
- **Franklin Delano Roosevelt** (1882-1945); the 32nd president of the United States.
- **Edward Teller** (1908-2003); a Hungarian physicist of Jewish origins, he was a member of America's Manhattan Engineer District, better known as the Manhattan Project, which researched and developed the first atomic bombs.
- **Benny Goodman** (1909-1986); an American jazz musician, clarinettist and bandleader, he was dubbed 'the King of Swing'.
- **Richard M. Nixon** (1913-1994); the 37th president of the United States.
- **Margaret Thatcher** (1925-2013); a British politician and leader of the Conservative Party, she held office as prime minister of the United Kingdom three times in succession, from 1979 to 1990, and earned the nickname of 'the Iron Lady'.
- **Patrick Stewart** (born in 1940); a British stage and screen actor whose filmography includes *Star Trek*.

- **Harrison Ford** (born in 1942); an American screen actor whose filmography includes the *Indiana Jones* series.
- **Hillary Clinton** (born in 1947); an America political activist, former Secretary of State and US senator, she is married to the 42nd president, Bill Clinton.
- **Al Gore** (born in 1948); the 45th vice-president of the United States.
- **Bill Gates** (born in 1955); an American entrepreneur and philanthropist, co-founder of the Microsoft company and one of the richest people in the world.
- **Whoopi Goldberg** (Caryn Elaine Johnson; born in 1955); an American screen actress, comedienne, political activist, writer and television host whose filmography includes *Ghost*, she has won some of America's most prestigious entertainment industry awards.
- **Steve Jobs** (1955-2011); an American entrepreneur and co-founder of the Apple company.
- **Quentin Tarantino** (born in 1963); an American director, screenwriter, cinematographer, producer and actor whose filmography includes *Kill Bill*.

The ID16™© Personality Types in a Nutshell

The Administrator (ESTJ)

Life motto: We'll get the job done!

Administrators are hard-working, responsible and extremely loyal. Energetic and decisive, they value order, stability, security and clear rules. They are matter-of-fact and businesslike, logical, rational and practical and possess the capability to assimilate large amounts of detailed information.

Superb organisers, they are intolerant of ineffectuality, wastefulness and slothfulness. True to their convictions and direct in their contact with others, they present their point of view decisively and openly express critical opinions, sometimes hurting other people as a result.

The *administrator*'s four natural inclinations:

- source of life energy: the exterior world
- mode of assimilating information: via the senses
- decision-making mode: the mind
- lifestyle: organised

Similar personality types:

- the Animator
- the Inspector
- the Practitioner

Statistical data:

- *administrators* constitute between ten and thirteen per cent of the global community
- men predominate among *administrators* (60 per cent)
- the United States is an example of a nation corresponding to the *administrator's* profile[3]

Find out more!

The Administrator. Your Guide to the ESTJ Personality Type by Jaroslaw Jankowski

---

[3] What this means is not that all the residents of the USA fall within this personality type, but that American society as a whole possesses a great many of the character traits typical of the *administrator*.

The Advocate (ESFJ)

Life motto: How can I help you?

Advocates are well-organised, energetic and enthusiastic. Practical, responsible and conscientious, they are sincere and exceptionally gregarious.

Advocates are perceptive of human feelings, emotions and needs. They value harmony and find criticism and conflict difficult to bear. With their sensitivity to any and every manifestation of injustice, prejudice or detriment to another, they are genuinely interested in other people's problems and take real delight in helping them and tending to their needs, while often neglecting their own. They have a tendency to do everything for others and can be vulnerable to manipulation.

The *advocate*'s four natural inclinations:

- source of life energy: the exterior world
- mode of assimilating information: via the senses
- decision-making mode: the heart
- lifestyle: organised

Similar personality types:

- the Presenter
- the Protector
- the Artist

Statistical data:

- *advocates* constitute between ten and thirteen per cent of the global community
- women predominate among *advocates* (70 per cent)
- Canada is an example of a nation corresponding to the *advocate's* profile

Find out more!

The Advocate. Your Guide to the ESFJ Personality Type by Jaroslaw Jankowski

The Animator (ESTP)

Life motto: Let's DO something!

Animators are energetic, active and enterprising. Fond of the company of others, they have the ability to enjoy the moment and are spontaneous, flexible and open to change.

Animators are inspirers and instigators, spurring others to act. Being logical, rational and pragmatic realists, they are wearied by abstract concepts and solutions for the future. Their focus is on solving concrete problems in the here and now. They have difficulties with organising and planning and can be impulsive, acting first and thinking later.

The *animator's* four natural inclinations:

- source of life energy: the exterior world
- mode of assimilating information: via the senses

- decision-making mode: the mind
- lifestyle: spontaneous

Similar personality types:

- the Administrator
- the Practitioner
- the Inspector

Statistical data:

- *animators* constitute between six and ten per cent of the global community
- men predominate among *animators* (60 per cent)
- Australia is an example of a nation corresponding to the *animator's* profile

Find out more!

The Animator. Your Guide to the ESTP Personality Type by Jaroslaw Jankowski

The Artist (ISFP)

Life motto: Let's create something!

Artists are sensitive, creative and original, with a sense of the aesthetic and natural artistic talents. Independent in character, they follow their own system of values and are optimistic in outlook, with a positive approach to life and an ability to enjoy the moment.

Helping others is a source of joy to them. They find abstract theories tedious and would rather create reality than talk about it, although starting on something new comes more easily to them than finishing what they have already started. They have difficulty in voicing their own desires and needs.

The *artist's* four natural inclinations:

- source of life energy: the interior world
- mode of assimilating information: via the senses
- decision-making mode: the heart
- lifestyle: spontaneous

Similar personality types:

- the Protector
- the Presenter
- the Advocate

Statistical data:

- *artists* constitute between six and nine per cent of the global community
- women predominate among *artists* (60 per cent)
- China is an example of a nation corresponding to the *artist's* profile

Find out more!

The Artist. Your Guide to the ISFP Personality Type by Jaroslaw Jankowski

The Counsellor (ENFJ)

Life motto: My friends are my world

Counsellors are optimistic, enthusiastic and quick-witted. Courteous and tactful, they have an extraordinary gift for empathy and find joy in acting for the good of others, with no thought of themselves. They have the ability to influence other people, inspiring them, eliciting their hidden potential and giving them faith in their own powers. Radiating warmth, they draw others to them and often help them in solving their personal problems.

Counsellors can be over-trusting and have a tendency to view the world through rose-tinted glasses. With their focus on other people, they often forget about their own needs.

The *counsellor's* four natural inclinations:

- source of life energy: the exterior world
- mode of assimilating information: intuition
- decision-making mode: the heart
- lifestyle: organised

Similar personality types:

- the Enthusiast
- the Mentor
- the Idealist

Statistical data:

- *counsellors* constitute between three and five per cent of the global community
- women predominate among *counsellors* (80 per cent)
- France is an example of a nation corresponding to the *counsellor's* profile

Find out more!

The Counsellor. Your Guide to the ENFJ Personality Type by Jaroslaw Jankowski

The Director (ENTJ)

Life motto: I'll tell you what you need to do.

Directors are independent, active and decisive. Rational, logical and creative, when they analyse problems they look at the wider picture and are able to foresee the future consequences of human activities. They are characterised by optimism and a healthy sense of their own worth and are capable of transforming theoretical concepts into concrete, practical plans of action.

Visionaries, mentors and organisers, *directors* possess natural leadership skills. Their powerful personalities and direct and critical style can often have an intimidating effect, causing them problems in their interpersonal relationships.

The *director's* four natural inclinations:

- source of life energy: the exterior world

- mode of assimilating information: intuition
- decision-making mode: the mind
- lifestyle: organised

Similar personality types:

- the Innovator
- the Strategist
- the Logician

Statistical data:

- *directors* constitute between two and five per cent of the global community
- men predominate among *directors* (70 per cent)
- Holland is an example of a nation corresponding to the *director's* profile

Find out more!

The Director. Your Guide to the ENTJ Personality Type by Jaroslaw Jankowski

The Enthusiast (ENFP)

Life motto: We'll manage!

Enthusiasts are energetic, enthusiastic and optimistic. Capable of enjoying life and looking ahead to the future, they are dynamic, quick-witted and creative. They have a liking for people in general, value honest and genuine relationships and are warm, sincere and emotional. Criticism is something they handle badly. With their gift for empathy and ability to perceive people's needs, feelings and motives, they both inspire others and infect them with their own enthusiasm.

They love to be at the centre of events and are flexible and capable of improvising. Their inclination leads towards idealistic notions. Being easily distracted, they have problems with seeing things through to the end.

The *enthusiast's* four natural inclinations:

- source of life energy: the exterior world
- mode of assimilating information: intuition
- decision-making mode: the heart
- lifestyle: spontaneous

Similar personality types:

- the Counsellor
- the Idealist
- the Mentor

Statistical data:

- *enthusiasts* constitute between five and eight per cent of the global community
- women predominate among *enthusiasts* (60 per cent)
- Italy is an example of a nation corresponding to the *enthusiast's* profile

Find out more!

The Enthusiast. Your Guide to the ENFP Personality Type by Jaroslaw Jankowski

The Idealist (INFP)

Life motto: We CAN live differently.

Idealists are sensitive, loyal, and creative. Living in accordance with the values they hold is of immense importance to them and they both manifest an interest in the reality of the spirit and delve deeply into the mysteries of life. Wrapped up in the world's problems and open to the needs of other people, they prize harmony and balance.

Idealists are romantic; not only are they able to show love, but they also need warmth and affection themselves. With their outstanding ability to read other people's feelings and emotions, they build healthy, profound and enduring relationships. They feel that they are on very shaky ground in situations of conflict and have no real resistance to stress and criticism.

The *idealist's* four natural inclinations:

- source of life energy: the interior world
- mode of assimilating information: intuition
- decision-making mode: the heart
- lifestyle: spontaneous

Similar personality types:

- the Mentor
- the Enthusiast
- the Counsellor

Statistical data:

- *idealists* constitute between one and four per cent of the global community
- women predominate among *idealists* (60 per cent)
- Thailand is an example of a nation corresponding to the *idealist's* profile

Find out more!

The Idealist. Your Guide to the INFP Personality Type by Jaroslaw Jankowski

The Innovator (ENTP)

Life motto: How about trying a different approach…?

Innovators are inventive, original and independent. Optimistic, energetic and enterprising, they are people of action who love being at the centre of events and solving 'insoluble' problems. Their thoughts are turned to the future and they are curious about the world and visionary by nature. Open to new concepts and ideas, they enjoy new experiences and experiments and have the ability to identify the connections between separate events.

Innovators are spontaneous, communicative and self-assured. However, they tend to overestimate their own possibilities and have problems with seeing things through to the end. They are also inclined to be impatient and to take risks.

The *innovator's* four natural inclinations:

- source of life energy: the exterior world
- mode of assimilating information: intuition
- decision-making mode: the mind
- lifestyle: spontaneous

Similar personality types:

- the Director
- the Logician
- the Strategist

Statistical data:

- *innovators* constitute between three and five per cent of the global community
- men predominate among *innovators* (70 per cent)
- Israel is an example of a nation corresponding to the *innovator's* profile

Find out more!

The Innovator. Your Guide to the ENTP Personality Type by Jaroslaw Jankowski

The Inspector (ISTJ)

Life motto: *Duty first.*

Inspectors are people who can always be counted on. Well-mannered, punctual, reliable, conscientious and responsible, when they give their word, they keep it. Being analytical, methodical, systematic and logical by nature, they tend be seen as serious, cold and reserved. They prize calm, stability and order, have no fondness for change and like clear principles and concrete rules.

Inspectors are hard-working, persevering and capable of seeing things through to the end. As perfectionists, they try to exercise control over everything within their sphere and are sparing in their praise. They also underrate the importance of other people's feelings and emotions.

The *inspector's* four natural inclinations:

- source of life energy: the interior world
- mode of assimilating information: via the senses
- decision-making mode: the mind
- lifestyle: organised

Similar personality types:

- the Practitioner
- the Administrator
- the Animator

Statistical data:

- *inspectors* constitute between six and ten per cent of the global community
- men predominate among *inspectors* (60 per cent)
- Switzerland is an example of a nation corresponding to the *inspector's* profile

Find out more!

The Inspector. Your Guide to the ISTJ Personality Type by Jaroslaw Jankowski

The Logician (INTP)

Life motto: Above all else, seek to discover the truths about the world.

Logicians are original, resourceful and creative. With a love for solving problems of a theoretical nature, they are analytical, quick-witted, enthusiastically disposed towards new concepts and have the ability to connect individual phenomena, educing general rules and theories from them. Logical, exact and inquiring, they are quick to spot incoherence and inconsistency.

Logicians are independent, sceptical of existing solutions and authorities, tolerant and open to new challenges. When immersed in thought, they will sometimes lose touch with the outside world.

The *logician's* four natural inclinations:

- source of life energy: the interior world

- mode of assimilating information: intuition
- decision-making mode: the mind
- lifestyle: spontaneous

Similar personality types:

- the Strategist
- the Innovator
- the Director

Statistical data:

- *logicians* constitute between two and three per cent of the global community;
- men predominate among *logicians* (80 per cent)
- India is an example of a nation corresponding to the *logician's* profile

Find out more!

The Logician. Your Guide to the INTP Personality Type by Jaroslaw Jankowski

The Mentor (INFJ)

Life motto: The world CAN be a better place!

Mentors are creative and sensitive. With their gaze fixed firmly on the future, they spot opportunities and potential imperceptible to others. Idealists and visionaries, they are geared towards helping people and are conscientious, responsible and, at one and the same time, courteous, caring and friendly. They strive to understand the mechanisms governing the world and view problems from a wide perspective.

Superb listeners and observers, *mentors* are characterised by their extraordinary empathy, intuition and trust of people and are capable of reading the feelings and emotions of others. They find criticism and conflict difficult to bear and can come across as enigmatic.

The *mentor's* four natural inclinations:

- source of life energy: the interior world
- mode of assimilating information: intuition
- decision-making mode: the heart
- lifestyle: organised

Similar personality types:

- the Idealist
- the Counsellor
- the Enthusiast

Statistical data:

- *mentors* constitute one per cent of the global community and are the most rarely occurring of the sixteen personality types
- women predominate among *mentors* (80 per cent)
- Norway is an example of a nation corresponding to the *mentor's* profile

Find out more!

The Mentor. Your Guide to the INFJ Personality Type by Jaroslaw Jankowski

The Practitioner (ISTP)

Life motto: Actions speak louder than words.

Practitioners are optimistic and spontaneous, with a positive approach to life. Reserved and independent, they hold true to their personal convictions and view external principles and norms with scepticism. They find abstract concepts and solutions for the future tiresome and would far rather roll up their sleeves and get to work on solving tangible and concrete problems.

Adapting well to new places and situations, they enjoy fresh challenges and risks and are capable of keeping a cool head in the face of threats and danger. Their general reticence and extreme reserve when it comes to expressing their opinions mean that other people may often find them impenetrable.

The *practitioner's* four natural inclinations:

- source of life energy: the interior world
- mode of assimilating information: via the senses
- decision-making mode: the mind
- lifestyle: spontaneous

Similar personality types:

- the Inspector
- the Animator
- the Administrator

Statistical data:

- *practitioners* constitute between six and nine per cent of the global community
- men predominate among *practitioners* (60 per cent)
- Singapore is an example of a nation corresponding to the *practitioner's* profile

Find out more!

The Practitioner. Your Guide to the ISTP Personality Type by Jaroslaw Jankowski

The Presenter (ESFP)

Life motto: Now is the perfect moment!

Presenters are optimistic, energetic and outgoing, with the ability to enjoy life and have fun to the full. Practical, flexible and spontaneous at one and the same time, they enjoy change and new experiences, coping badly with solitude, stagnation and routine.

With their liking for being at the centre of attention, they are natural-born actors and their speaking abilities arouse the interest and enthusiasm of their listeners. Focused as they are on the present moment, they will sometimes lose sight of their long-term aims and can also have problems with foreseeing the consequences of their actions.

The *presenter's* four natural inclinations:

- source of life energy: the exterior world
- mode of assimilating information: via the senses
- decision-making mode: the heart
- lifestyle: spontaneous

Similar personality types:

- the Advocate
- the Artist
- the Protector

Statistical data:

- *presenters* constitute between eight and thirteen per cent of the global community
- women predominate among *presenters* (60 per cent)
- Brazil is an example of a nation corresponding to the *presenter's* profile

Find out more!

The Presenter. Your Guide to the ESFP Personality Type by Jaroslaw Jankowski

The Protector (ISFJ)

Life motto: Your happiness matters to me.

Protectors are sincere, warm-hearted, unassuming, trustworthy and extraordinarily loyal. With their ability to perceive people's needs and their desire to help them, they will always put others first. Practical, well-organised and gifted with both an eye and a memory for detail, they are responsible, hard-working, patient, persevering and capable of seeing things through to the end.

Protectors set great store by tranquillity, stability and friendly relations with others and are skilled at building bridges between people. By the same token, they find conflict and criticism difficult to bear. Given their powerful sense of duty and their constant readiness to come to the aid of others, they can end up being used by people.

The *protector's* four natural inclinations:

- source of life energy: the interior world
- mode of assimilating information: via the senses
- decision-making mode: the heart
- lifestyle: organised

Similar personality types:

- the Artist
- the Advocate
- the Presenter

Statistical data:

- *protectors* constitute between eight and twelve per cent of the global population
- women predominate among *protectors* (70 per cent)
- Sweden is an example of a nation corresponding to the *protector's* profile

Find out more!

The Protector. Your Guide to the ISFJ Personality Type by Jaroslaw Jankowski

The Strategist (INTJ)

Life motto: I can certainly improve this.

Strategists are independent and outstandingly individualistic, with an immense seam of inner energy. Creative, inventive and resourceful, others perceive them as competent, self-assured and, at one and the same time, distant and enigmatic. No matter what they turn their attention to, they will always look at the bigger picture and they have a driving urge to improve the world around them and set it in order.

Well-organised, responsible, critical and demanding, they are difficult to knock off balance – and just as hard to please to the full. Reading the emotions and feelings of others is something they find very problematic.

The *strategist's* four natural inclinations:

- source of life energy: the interior world
- mode of assimilating information: intuition
- decision-making mode: the mind
- lifestyle: organised

Similar personality types:

- the Logician
- the Director
- the Innovator

Statistical data:

- *strategists* constitute between one and two per cent of the global community
- men predominate among *strategists* (80 per cent)
- Finland is an example of a nation corresponding to the *strategist's* profile

Find out more!

The Strategist. Your Guide to the INTJ Personality Type by Jaroslaw Jankowski

Additional information

The four natural inclinations

1. THE DOMINANT SOURCE OF LIFE
   ENERGY

   a. THE EXTERIOR WORLD
      People who draw their energy
      from outside. They need activity
      and contact with others and find
      being alone for any length of time
      hard to bear.

   b. THE INTERIOR WORLD
      People who draw their energy
      from their inner world. They need
      quiet and solitude and feel drained

when they spend any length of time in a group.

2. THE DOMINANT MODE OF ASSIMILATING INFORMATION

    a. VIA THE SENSES
        People who rely on the five senses and are persuaded by facts and evidence. They have a liking for methods and practices which are tried and tested and prefer concrete tasks and are realists who trust in experience.

    b. VIA INTUITION
        People who rely on the sixth sense and are driven by what they 'feel in their bones'. They have a liking for innovative solutions and problems of a theoretical nature and are characterised by a creative approach to their tasks and the ability to predict.

3. THE DOMINANT DECISION-MAKING MODE

    a. THE MIND
        People who are guided by logic and objective principles. They are critical and direct in expressing their opinions.

b. THE HEART
    People who are guided by their
    feelings and values. They long for
    harmony and mutual
    understanding with others.

4. THE DOMINANT LIFESTYLE

a. ORGANISED
    People who are conscientious and
    organised. They value order and
    like to operate according to plan.

b. SPONTANEOUS
    People who are spontaneous and
    value freedom of action. They live
    for the moment and have no
    trouble finding their feet in new
    situations.

The approximate percentage of each personality type in the world population

Personality Type:	Proportion:
• The Administrator (ESTJ):	10-13%
• The Advocate (ESFJ):	10-13%
• The Animator (ESTP):	6-10%
• The Artist (ISFP):	6-9%
• The Counsellor (ENFJ):	3-5 %
• The Director (ENTJ):	2-5%
• The Enthusiast (ENFP):	5-8%

- The Idealist (INFP):   1-4%
- The Innovator (ENTP):   3-5%
- The Inspector (ISTJ):   6-10%
- The Logician (INTP):   2-3%
- The Mentor (INFJ):   ca. 1%
- The Practitioner (ISTP):   6-9%
- The Presenter (ESFP):   8-13%
- The Protector (ISFJ):   8-12%
- The Strategist (INTJ):   1-2%

The approximate percentage of women and men of each personality type in the world population

Personality Type: **Women / Men:**

- The Administrator (ESTJ):   40% / 60%
- The Advocate (ESFJ):   70% / 30%
- The Animator (ESTP):   40% / 60%
- The Artist (ISFP):   60% / 40%
- The Counsellor (ENFJ):   80% / 20%
- The Director (ENTJ):   30% / 70%
- The Enthusiast (ENFP):   60% / 40%
- The Idealist (INFP):   60% / 40%
- The Innovator (ENTP):   30% / 70%
- The Inspector (ISTJ):   40% / 60%
- The Logician (INTP):   20% / 80%
- The Mentor (INFJ):   80% / 20%
- The Practitioner (ISTP):   40% / 60%
- The Presenter (ESFP):   60% / 40%
- The Protector (ISFJ):   70% / 30%
- The Strategist (INTJ):   20% / 80%

Bibliography

- Arraj, Tyra & Arraj, James: *Tracking the Elusive Human, Volume 1: A Practical Guide to C.G. Jung's Psychological Types, W.H. Sheldon's Body and Temperament Types and Their Integration*, Inner Growth Books, 1988

- Arraj, James: *Tracking the Elusive Human, Volume 2: An Advanced Guide to the Typological Worlds of C. G. Jung, W.H. Sheldon, Their Integration, and the Biochemical Typology of the Future*, Inner Growth Books, 1990

- Berens, Linda V.; Cooper, Sue A.; Ernst, Linda K.; Martin, Charles R.; Myers, Steve; Nardi, Dario; Pearman, Roger R.; Segal, Marci; Smith, Melissa: *A Quick Guide to the 16 Personality Types in Organizations: Understanding Personality Differences in the Workplace*, Telos Publications, 2002

- Geier, John G. & Downey, E. Dorothy: *Energetics of Personality*, Aristos Publishing House, 1989

- Hunsaker, Phillip L. & Alessandra, Anthony J.: *The Art of Managing People*, Simon and Schuster, 1986

- Jung, Carl Gustav: *Psychological Types (The Collected Works of C. G. Jung, Vol. 6)*, Princeton University Press, 1976

- Kise, Jane A. G.; Stark, David & Krebs Hirsch, Sandra: *Lifekeys: Discover Who You Are*, Bethany House, 2005
- Kroeger, Otto & Thuesen, Janet: *Type Talk or How to Determine Your Personality Type and Change Your Life*, Delacorte Press, 1988
- Lawrence, Gordon: *People Types and Tiger Stripes*, Center for Applications of Psychological Type, 1993
- Lawrence, Gordon: *Looking at Type and Learning Styles*, Center for Applications of Psychological Type, 1997
- Maddi, Salvatore R.: *Personality Theories: A Comparative Analysis*, Waveland, 2001
- Martin, Charles R.: *Looking at Type: The Fundamentals Using Psychological Type To Understand and Appreciate Ourselves and Others*, Center for Applications of Psychological Type, 2001
- Meier C.A.: Personality: *The Individuation Process in the Light of C. G. Jung's Typology*, Daimon Verlag, 2007
- Pearman, Roger R. & Albritton, Sarah: *I'm Not Crazy, I'm Just Not You: The Real Meaning of the Sixteen Personality Types*, Davies-Black Publishing, 1997
- Segal, Marci: Creativity and Personality Type: *Tools for Understanding and Inspiring the Many Voices of Creativity*, Telos Publications, 2001
- Sharp, Daryl: Personality Type: *Jung's Model of Typology*, Inner City Books, 1987
- Spoto, Angelo: *Jung's Typology in Perspective*, Chiron Publications, 1995
- Tannen, Deborah: *You Just Don't Understand*, William Morrow and Company, 1990
- Thomas, Jay C. & Segal, Daniel L.: *Comprehensive Handbook of Personality and Psychopathology, Personality and Everyday Functioning*, Wiley, 2005
- Thomson, Lenore: *Personality Type: An Owner's Manual*, Shambhala, 1998
- Tieger, Paul D. & Barron-Tieger Barbara: *Just Your Type: Create the Relationship You've Always Wanted Using the Secrets of Personality Type*, Little, Brown and Company, 2000
- Von Franz, Marie-Louise & Hillman, James: *Lectures on Jung's Typology*, Continuum International Publishing Group, 1971

www.ingramcontent.com/pod-product-compliance
Lightning Source LLC
Chambersburg PA
CBHW031208020426
42333CB00013B/848